Daughter
Lover
Mother
Crone

Poems by
Julie Quinn

Printed in the United States of America

ISBN: 978-1-968563-76-9

Acknowledgments

Weeds – First published in *Minnesota Monthly*, May 1996.

Autumn – First published in *Minnesota Monthly*, October 1998.

Love Lessons – First published in *Kouroo,* Summer 2000.

Dedication

To Mary Cassidy,

Thank you for being my writing buddy, my first reader, my inspiration, and my friend.

Table of Contents

DAUGHTER 1

   I Am Eleven 2

   Bad Seed 3

   Rats to the Party 4

   Mother, You Raised a Dog-Hearted Child 5

   Form Letter #223 6

   Real Life 7

   Deja Vu 8

   The Great Forgetting 9

   Other Questions You Might Ask 10

LOVER 11

   Weeds 12

   Night Vision 13

   Love Lessons 14

   Pear-shaped Women 15

   Six Shakey Nouns 16

   Panther 17

   Late Love 18

   A Chain of Definitions 19

   Marriage 20

MOTHER 21

   Still A Child Inside 22

   I Often Dream 23

   Morning Chores 25

   This Day You Are Having Right Now 26

   Mouse 27

   Now That You Are A Poet 28

   How You Get Your Gas 29

This Is Why Poetry Exists.. 30

Eros & Agape... 31

CRONE **33**

Autumn... 34

Recluse 35

Who Would Not Be A Monster 36

Crazy Joy.. 37

Musings 38

We're at That Age 39

Loneliness 40

Ganesh and Shiva Waltz 41

DAUGHTER

I Am Eleven

I want mother to wake up.
The day cannot begin
Until she emerges from her room.
I know better than to disturb her.

The trees are rustling.
I want to be outside
But I lie quietly in my room,
Waiting.

If I rise before she goes to work,
She will have me fetch things for her.
Whatever I bring her will be wrong.
She knows I pretend to sleep
Until she is gone.

I count my breaths
Until she wakes,
Until she leaves.

She lies in bed,
Then sits at the kitchen table,
Counting hers too.

Bad Seed

Forget eternity.
Only the crease in
Your mother's forehead is timeless.
Only your father's sigh
Lasts longer than the pharaohs' tombs.
Their disappointment in you
Is the dense core of the earth,
The hot, hard center of
Every ill wind which
Bears your name.

Still, the gravity of blood
Holds you in their orbit.
Love and hope
Keep you circling,
Keep you paging
Through the family album,
Keep you digging
Back to a time
When a couple with
Unlined faces
Stood behind
A freckled child,
And smiled.

Rats to the Party

Mom came to my party.
Of course, she did.
Bearing a party platter the size of New York.
Leafy greens, crudités, dozens of kinds of imported
Meats and cheeses.
She put half my food back in the kitchen
Just to make room.

And nobody touched it,
Cowed as they were by its perfection.
They kept talking, avoided
Making eye contact with the buffet,
While she went off to sulk in the corner.

Feeling obligated to be grateful,
I went to load up a plate,
Only to find a scaly tail
Slithering round the cheese ball, and
Three rats lurking in the kale.

I turned to where mom was pouting.
"Mom, you brought rats to my party."

She sniffed.
"You never appreciate anything I do for you."

Mother, You Raised a Dog-Hearted Child

See how she laps up your attention,
Lays her head upon your knee,
Looks up with pleading eyes.

Love me, oh love me,
And I will forgive
The belts and the beatings,
Each mean-spirited kick of your tongue.

Still, there comes a day when
Even a dog's had too much.
She snaps her leash, and
Never looks back.

Don't call her to heel—
She'll go for your throat.

Form Letter #223

Dear (mother, father, sibling, spouse, or other);

I wish to thank you
For your generous advice
On how to live
My life.
Please do not think me ungrateful,
But I must regretfully
Refuse to take it.

After years of thinking things over,
I have finally realized
That I could never make your mistakes
As well as you have -
No matter how hard I tried,
And that in attempting to do so,
I would make my life
Just a pale imitation of yours.

Perhaps, in pursuing my own errors
With the same passion and enthusiasm
I observed while watching you,
I will fail
In a way spectacular and loud,
Eventually achieving something
Which would make you
Proud.

Real Life

This is where your real life begins:
Not at graduation, but
At the lost job;
At the curve where your car leaves the road;
At the moment of blackness
After the unseen man hits you with the pipe;
At the instant the one thing
You never dreamed could happen, happens.

Until then, you never knew you were blind,
Or how dark darkness could be.
You didn't know the meaning of the word brave,
And didn't know you had it in you
To put one foot in front of the other,
To keep pushing onward,
Angry and afraid,
But still willing to keep going....

Always willing to move ahead.

Deja Vu

You dreamed the moment when you remembered
You had dreamed that moment.

And in your dream you said:
I dreamt this before.

Of course you hadn't,
But when you really said it,
You already had.

You felt light headed.
You didn't know whether you
Had already dreamed this moment,
Or you were still dreaming it.

You felt as if you were caught between two mirrors.
You could see yourself dreaming dreams
Of dreaming dreams into infinity.

Is there even a difference between dreams and reality?
You remember dreaming this question—
But not the answer.

The Great Forgetting

In my dream I had
A father I'd never had before,
Who loved me. And a mother
With long gray hair and a patient smile.
He was dying and hugged me goodbye.
I squeezed him back, but I turned my face
Because of his tobacco breath.

"Don't let them forget me," he said.

But how could we forget?
As long as we live, we'll be saying things like
"Rise and shine, greet the new day!" or
"What your mother doesn't know, won't hurt her."

"It's you who are going into the great forgetting,"
I reminded him.

But he swore he never could, never would,
And I sighed.

Eternity would feel so long
If he never let go.

Other Questions You Might Ask

If there is no God,
Who gave us the gift of terminal illness and old age?
Who else knows how we hunger to love
Our parents unconditionally,
Despite everything,
The way they once loved us -
Cleaning drool from our chins,
Finding our mouths with the spoon,
Wiping our bottoms,
Even when we didn't know who we were,
Even when we didn't know who they were,
Even when we would smile at just anyone
Who would answer our cry?

What if this is your last chance
To nap with your mother on a plaid blanket
In the late afternoon while the light fades?

LOVER

Weeds

Wildness
Springs uncontrolled
From the cracks in your life.

Like nettles between the tulips,
Like deer grazing among the cows
In a field outside of Tomah,

Prickly and unexpected,
Like that long pause
After he says your name.

Night Vision

Wanton that she is,
Your cat sits in the moonlit window
Licking herself.

She will not help you
Navigate jealousy.

Your eyes must make their own way
Through the darkness.
You turn them to her but
She gazes at the street where
Her next lover waits.

He aches, but does not yet know
He aches for her.

Love Lessons

It comes down to emptiness
This word love. No substance.
Not even the thing itself.
Just a finger pointing across the room.

A simple "I love you," tossed carelessly, flies
Like an arrow to the heart of your doubt,
Blows you from your safe cushion,
Knocks Dogen's rules of *zazen* (and life) from your mind:

Sit in a quiet place. Do not disturb others.
(Especially the one whose shoulder pillows your head)
Do not be disturbed by others.
(Especially by their words when thoughtless
But not meant to harm.)

Even in a room of five hundred, sit by yourself.
(It is good to consider love's many *koans*:
Whose hand is it, that cups your face in the dark?
Which breath do you draw, yours, or your beloved's?)

Apply yourself through the rising and
Falling of inexhaustible desires
Until you see that even when a lover
Waits between your sheets,
There is only one in the room when you finally surrender,
Dropping fear like a robe at the foot of the bed.

Pear-shaped Women

They call them Venuses,
These palm-sized figurines,
Fossil fruit from Europe
Bearing exotic names:
Willendorf,
Laussel,
Lespugue.
They hint of the garden:
Golden skin over rounded orbs
Teeth biting tender flesh,
Sweet pear juice
Running down
Your chin.

Six Shakey Nouns

My love is like six shakey nouns and
A transitive verb.
It is an irrational number
Written on a mobius strip.

Have you ever met a stranger who smiled, saying
"Nice day, isn't it?"
Only to have your heart answer,
"You're here at last."

That's not a beginning.
It's a reunion.

Maybe we don't need to do anything.
Maybe we just need to breathe together,
Wherever we are,
Near or far,
To feel the chord between us tremble,
To send ripples into infinity.

You, me, we.
He, she, they.
Are.

Panther

It is the eyes,
Not just looking,
Watching,
From the edges—

It is the snapped twig;
The rustle,
The surge of muscle
Through the trees—

It is the shadow,
The hunger,
The waiting
For what must come—

That makes you gaze
At the forest.

That makes you linger on paths
Where you do not belong.

That makes you linger on paths—

That makes you linger—

That makes you bare your throat
And lie down.

Late Love

These are the first days of fall
Come creeping into knees and back
Throbbing a thousand worries
Riding his shoulders strong but ready
To throw off the load pitch it
And just walk off windward leeward
Any way but into that gaping maw
Of duty ready to chew him up
Munch crunch slurp suck
Until empty shell of dead tarantula
He crumbles pile of dust when poked
And the last thing he hungers after
Yearns for hunts down in his dreams
Is more burdensome yak yak yak rolling him
Silly putty back into its plastic egg
No escape he can't
He mustn't
He will not do it
No more not one more soul
Putting the sold sign on his life
But then she slips slantwise
Sneaky into his arms
Lays her hand on his cheek caresses
And he thinks of sirens witches gypsies
Evil spell drowning he doesn't want
Can't resist still surrenders
When she says,
"Rest."

A Chain of Definitions

Plight your Troth
Braid your truths together.
Pledge your faith and loyalty
In *Marriage* or *Engagement*,
An intimate union,
The act of being occupied
With each other,
Of making an appointment,
A moral commitment
To be *Helpmates*,
Partners,
Companions in dance,
Skipping lightly
Through the paces
Of your lives.

Marriage

Like the art of blowing wine goblets – only hotter.
In this furnace, you work against time and gravity,
Against collapse: the liquid leaning-in of glass, and
Its tendency to shatter in icy air.

MOTHER

Still A Child Inside

Last night I dreamt my Nana rang the bell.
She'd read on Facebook that I
Needed someone to watch my children.

That's weird. It's the second time
Someone posted I need a sitter . . .
And I'm only a kid myself.

Just then Mom came in, a squalling infant in her arms.
"This one won't shut up," she said,
Thrusting the child at me.

As I took the baby, I saw a little boy,
Three years old, propelling a monster truck
Across the rug. Brrroooom! Brrrooommm!

Oh, I thought.
When did that happen?

I Often Dream

I.

I often dream
That men in dark suits are coming
To arrest my father, my sisters, or me. I hide
In the lilacs. The others, together, somewhere hide
In the darkness. I can save them
If I let the G-men find me,
But I sit in the bushes,
Unable to move.

II.

I often dream
That my father and I are driving
Across a bridge, burning
Behind us. When we reach
The end, we must drive down
A spiral pedestrian ramp.
Around every bend, a boy
On a bicycle swerves
Into our path, swerves
Out just in time, pedals
Into the flames.

III.

I often dream
That I drive a woodland path, going
To my initiation, don't see
The turn, lock
The brakes, skid between two trees.
Cars pile up behind me:
Mom's, Dad's, sisters'. Some one hits

My drivers side rear fender. A dog limps
From in front of my car, dragging
It's left rear leg. One sister screams
"You've killed a little girl, look!"
But I can't look, knowing
I hit nothing, and knowing
There's a white pinafore child lying
Beneath my wheels.

IV.

I often dream
That I left my infant son in London
Where he grows up wild, and hides
From me when I try to find him.
He's mad that I abandoned him,
So I put the word out,
"Tell him that I will
Never stop looking
For him."

Morning Chores *(Homage to Robert Lax)*

Seed, seed
Feed, feed
Water, water
Clean.

Spaniels
Doberman
Cockatiel
Lizard
Tree frog
Fish.

Seed, seed
Feed, feed
Water, water
Clean.

Time for a cup
Time for a cup
Time for a cup
Of coffee
Time for a cup
Of coffee.

Before waking up
Before waking up
Before waking up
The kids, the kids
Before waking up
The kids.

Seed, seed
Feed, feed
Water, water
Clean.

Open the cupboard
Open the cupboard
Open the cupboard
And see
And see.

Dishes, cups and saucers
Dishes, cups and saucers
Enough to feed
Enough to feed
A threshing crew
A threshing crew
Enough to feed
A threshing crew.

Seed, seed
Feed, feed
Water, water
Clean.

This Day You Are Having Right Now

You need to come back again and again to your breath, to the day you are actually having.

— Mel Weitsman, San Francisco Zen Center

Not the day you wish you were having,
Enthroned in your favorite chair,
Book, music, cup of tea, and dog at your feet.

Not the day you think you should be having,
Praised by a boss who finally sees your contribution
To the company's success.

Not the day you could be having somewhere tomorrow,
Supervisor, or manager, or even CEO,
Anything but a lowly worker bee.

But this day right now,
The computer before you,
The dishes in the sink,

The children calling "M-o-m!"

Mouse

When you look for the mouse in a moment of bravery,
Ready to stare down the nightmare you know
Is only inches of quivering fur and a tail,
You can never find it.

Only when you are up to your elbows in pastry flour,
Or scrounging the pantry for the last of the kidney beans,
A shadow darts along the edge of sight and visions
Of breeding pestilence leave you gasping.

It is only a mouse. Everyone gets them. No need for shame.
Yet when the minister's wife comes to tea,
You try not to rattle your cup in its saucer
As your silent disgrace noses from the baseboard
Then boldly saunters out to preen its whiskers in the sun.

Now That You Are A Poet

Family,
Friends,
Even the bedroom bureau,
Once so transparent,
Assumes an inscrutable mask,
Unwilling to be
Used.

How You Get Your Gas

A truck loads in a bay in a rack at a terminal or refinery, top or bottom loading, vapor recovery, *Scully* ground. Card-in, and pick a blend: gasoline or fuel oil; high sulfur, low or ultra-low; on-road or off; dyed or clear; premium, mid-grade, or no-lead; oxygenated or straight. Punch in the numbers; hit the start; positive displacement or turbine meter; *Brooks, Smith or Accuload;* six to eight hundred gallons a minute. Do not switch load number one fuel oil into a compartment which last held gasoline, or the whole place may go boom. Drivers stay by your trucks while loading is in progress. Anyone caught jamming the dead man switch will be permanently banned from this facility. Eight thousand gallons of fuel into a trailer riding piggyback on a *Mack* tractor, or a *Peterbilt*; hope it doesn't tip; hope it doesn't jack-knife; hope the roads are dry; hope the brakes hold; hope no one cuts you off – *Jesus Christ! Not so close! This rig is a 32-ton bomb, or an environmental disaster waiting to happen* – hope no one is parked over the storage tanks at the station. Remove the lids; stick the tanks; dump the product; walk out the hoses; get the manager to sign the manifest. Don't forget the orange safety cones. Three, maybe four or five runs a shift; seven days a week; even on weekends; even on holidays; even on the night the driver's son stars in the school play. Slip into a seat just as the auditorium darkens and the curtain lifts.

This Is Why Poetry Exists

Because the men at the oil terminal,
Drivers and pipeline employees all
Get tired of debating whether Monet would paint
Tank farms instead of haystacks in
Alexandria, Minnesota.

Tank farms are eyesores.
No one would paint them.

No. They're canvasses,
Perfect for the study of light.

What they really want is a chance
To record the details of their lives.
A chance for a little friendly competition.
A chance to see who can write the best poem:

Sunlight on Storage Tanks

Eros & Agape

The world is what it is.
Nothing sacred.
But still we struggle.

Reaching towards grace, we drag
Trees, stars, mountains
Behind us.

As if the milky smell of a baby's breath
Isn't already heaven.

CRONE

Autumn

Today we pick pumpkins at the roadside stand,
Dried sunflowers and cornstalks
Leaning against a silvered wagon.
Just over the horizon you are a cracked leather mitt
Pulled from a chest for your grandson's inspection,
And I am a faded afghan in the new baby's room.
Further down the road we are yellowed photographs
Stored in a basement box.
Then names read backwards in a rearview mirror.
Today we pull our jackets close against the wind.
Sunlight slants across stubbly fields.
Our breath rises white before it disappears.

Recluse

For a long time I have lived in a narrow room.
The hibiscus bloom lasts only for a day, but
Flowers again each morning.
I ask only for the twittering of the sparrows
Outside my window.
Is that too much?
Yet the bobcat's growl and the whoosh of the crane
Pound against my pane.

Lock the door.
Close the blinds.
This world is more than I can bear.

Ugliness and beauty?
I use my skin as a filter against them.
And still the universe barges in,
Hurling a gold and violet sunrise
Against my white walls.

Who Would Not Be A Monster

Is there anything in the natural world you would give up?
And how would you choose between
A blond cornfield rustling in the slant of winter light, or
A meadow scattered with rolls of hay
Like giant playthings left carelessly about?
The flaming yellow of poplar and ash, or
The incandescent orange of a maple or a liquid amber tree?
Silver fog against a darkening wood, or
Jagged peaks piercing a turquoise sky?
A ribbon of road unfurling across undulating hills, or
A meandering track through a bamboo forest where
Every bend leads to another secret room of silent trees?

Of course, you would want to devour the world,
To drink the oceans dry in hungry gulps
As if there would never be enough to slake your thirst.
You would have to look and look and look and look,
To fight sleep like a child who is afraid
She might miss something even better than
Everything else that has come before.

And who would not be a monster?
Who would not breakfast on beauty?
Eat glory like bonbons as the sun went down?
Who would be so humble that they would not
Wrap majesty around them like a blanket?
Or think to themselves:

This.
This was all for me.

Crazy Joy

We were building hymns of praise to the universe
But some of the bricks were glazed and others unglazed.
The congregants were grumbling amongst themselves,
Wanting their words to be chanted forever, while
Others wanted to know their peons would turn to dust
As all things do.

None were happy.

The zendo is filthy and the teacher doesn't see it.
He parrots the words of his teachers,
But well enough that some of his students understand.
It is a gift, even if he can't unwrap it.
They bring him tea and call him master
to soothe his loss.

On the corner stands a man with a saxophone
Who plays like an angel on weed.
Crazy joy peels out of him
Turning walking meditation into a New Orleans parade.
The walls vibrate with joy, but even the unbaked bricks
Do not crumble.

The grumblers stop their litany to listen.
Someone picks up a dust rag.
Another a broom.
The ones on the threshold of leaving turn
To see that the hall is big enough after all.
Everyone can find a place for their song.

Musings

What if we were angels making music as well as messes?

What if our notes were glazed ceramic tiles
Gleaming in the light?
As well as terra cotta bricks
Crumbling to dust around us?

We all want to be dazzled by
Something that will not last forever.

That's what makes it precious...
And painful.

Would eternity feel like eternity if
We had not lost so much?

What if to praise God means to sing the blues?

We're at That Age

And now we have reached the plane
Of missed goodbyes.
We, the widows and the orphans,
Must brace ourselves
To dig our children's graves.
For no one knows
Who will disappear,
Or when.

Your best friend,
Jogging just ahead,
Dips below the horizon.
No matter how hard you run,
You never catch up.

Let no one be alone again.
Let us all join hands like
Children playing in the dark.
Hold tight as
We move across the grass.
Cry if someone drops out
But do not stop.
Take the hand
Reaching across the gap,
And go on.

Loneliness

The full moon slides a gentle finger
Across two, half-filled, double beds.
Old lovers dream they are not yet alone.

Ganesh and Shiva Waltz

Everything born
Eventually dies,
So put on your happy clothes
And dance.